# 8th Avenue

## STEFAN BRECHT

SPUYTEN DUYVIL
*New York City*

ISBN 1-933132-23-X

Library of Congress Cataloging-in-Publication Data

Brecht, Stefan, 1924-

8th Avenue / Stefan Brecht.

p. cm.

ISBN-13: 978-1-933132-23-5

ISBN-10: 1-933132-23-X

1. New York (N.Y.)--Poetry. I. Title: Eighth Avenue. II. Title.

PS3552.R3618A613 2005

811'.54--dc22

2005028405

Printed in Canada

*How soon could we regret the pavement's stone. The trash.*
*In eye of hurricane we stand content.*

8TH AVENUE POEMS

# 7 : 4 5    A . M .

the low-stress rumble of the ancient vans

idling pleasurably under the clouds with Latin names

the tiny locks as yet like hearts

silent on the storefront's metal veils

the driver frozen in his cabin's dreams

When as yet down toward the Hudson River, Stygian night prevails,

at my right the cameo of the roof tops ascends, azure,

a broken cup's vision of milk.

On my left shoulder I seem to bear the burden of sleepinesses spread

                                        throughout the houses,

my right shoulder is thrust into the coming of the light.

I heel but evening will right my gait

my dawn-blessed shoulder pressed into the neon.

the ladies of the court traipse
the silk of the green corn shimmering in their hair
on their tightly packed feet
across the palace floor
swaying, each in a cloud of a myriad tiny hearts

diminishing in its silent force
tree by tree
the wind blows down the block from around the corner

where the boy ladies of the night
in a theater of post-prom gaiety
writhe under their cakes of mascara
in sex change heedless
of the wind

to which every tree responds
according to the extent of its growth

above the towers
the morning star's ambiguous white
pocks the brilliance of the sky
by its minute scintillation
signs out the tenement
in which the son is born
in a side street's picture is caught
incensed by a dark Buick's cracked rock
my feet's ornament for a couple of blocks.
The skyline rising
wipes it out

The old cleaning lady beyond the door of glass
on her sore feet carefully checks the door
to reassure herself that it is still locked,
seeming to hold on to it

in the narrow trough of their shop the three Koreans stoop
amidst the brilliance of their sun-colored fruit, shades
smoothly releasing the energy
of the order of their fruit

in the bakeshop's white and silver
the young immigrant woman's movements
softly raise the pitcher, holding it
framed in the door to the kitchen
white in her white embrace

she is washing the onyx wall of the shop's entrance

her wet mop swishing

over her intelligent face, and her body

not quite as taut, and stouter

than once it was

# 8TH AVENUE BLACK MAN.

he is phoning and I notice

that he stands, unusually outside

the plastic shields' embrasure

a whole figure, ungesturing, a man

and as I pass I notice

in his face the loving hands of many mothers

a quiet kindness

of his eyes.

I was astounded to note on the subway grating the skins near the mango pit

were orange skins but then reflected

that two people had eaten different kinds of fruit together

in the course of the night. Yet where were

the peelings of the mango?

the tiny jacks of the bird's twitter

raise the white sky.  Sunday burgeons,

the small paradise

of the employed.

Emerging sudden on the Sabbath

above the bric-a-brac of anxious brick

the corporation, giant watchman, gathers

its loins in monolith of

bankruptcy.  Swathed in the slipstream rags of history

it lifts to flight, the Pan American! the avenue.

Awash in silent gamma rays the dawn bright brick hull soars

in free flight past its watchman,

resplendent missile of decrepitude.

As cool yet I come up the street, legs banter

in the angle between wall and sidewalk, having a good time

from the chairs stacked in the plateglass,

cupless roughening bywalking sweetglance

at a small table

in the cool morning

outside the closed café

on the deserted avenue

the couple banters

with nothing on the table

their charm a matter of apprehension

as I pass,

appreciation withdrawn: the town is big.

Walking with careful dignity over their bellies

slitmouth to jobs that start before nine from the subway

I read their immense victory not in their stubborn short of old men's faces

but in the old men's now that it's spring thrice-coated sleeping off seated

their wine jags on the steps of the bank whose insignium was before it went broke

the golden honey bee.

Mine eyes so much devour in paint, rust, metal

my ears, the coming to my head sideways

of sound me surprises as sudden

the fantail subway whirling up through the grates

the coolness breath of the fragile clatter of the engines

envelops me

the traffic's wavebeat making the lights,

grace of bosom line to nipple

the dip as drivers morning conscious slow for coming green,

flight surr even of through-run

uplift press of the bird soar

delicate hiss, beating the light change

plumround ripeness of stop. And through the tapestry a birdshot honking soprano, quite

small.


This of such nature texture, the feel of sea

within the which my swimming eye espies the morsels

that  testify to me.

Alongside of this tree-shaped park's verticals, partly,

in my Sunday morning's accelerating whiteness

in the blackness of their Saturday night the Negroes stand

told apart  by their raised arms' argument.

# Sunday Morning

on mailbox soars the eagle miniscule

the pigeons strut in trash of winds

aflutter flares atop the nation's emblem

a furtive back shields furtive bladder

from anthills stacked of words a twitter rises

the Lord is dead but Pilate lives.

# D A W N

"Opalescence" means a glow next to a body like that of light itself
nestled so intimately close to the skin or other surface of the body
it seems a sky of odors—the odors of trees, of extensive meadows,
the odor of the moon—and still and yet that body's own, the earth's,
                                                    its opening up and giving itself over
in arms' fullness, from the heart, revealing that lo! yes it has no heart,
                                        its center
that giving of itself over in entirety outwards from the heart in opalescence.

It's six a.m. and the sun is rising Memorial Day

on him reading on this Monday Sunday's ads, seated carefully

back to wall, legs crossed, on the pavement, on another two pages,

his finger tracing down the column, facing the street stretching

the road of asphalt and the two strips of concrete concave and slightly shiny

                              running in the morning

not endlessly but far past him someone that you might say really has no place to go

but in the American Dream will get his shit together and start trudging

looking for that job to-morrow down the endless street, or more likely not

but looks neat, hair parted, the short line of his finger out from the wall

back toward his stomach and the wall slowly tracing the black letters

extended into the far longer line of the street stretching past him like

                              a banquet table, arching

past him from north to south, swelling as though beneath it rested a lily pond

and the avenue were a Chinese bridge, ornate and carved over its darkness, and he

the scholarly poet

gathering his wits in the early morning

on his estate.

this here colored man walks

in a countryman's gait, shambling

down the avenue on a Wednesday morning

his mule invisible, even dressed, blue,

for the occasion of his appearance in a pink dreamland

spreading about his big feet.

the sun's wind about their eyes chastises these children

in their dark glasses, hastily formed out of the dark asphalt

in self-defense, lashes them as they turn in their confusion,

a checkering about their cheekbones, the flutter of April, May preening

in their play brief, dark and golden

the children of the poor, the

too many.

in the mixture of stone as in a fruitbowl red and yellow

the silence of Saturday rests

shivering on the subway's rumbling grate,

crisscrossed by street signs, slowly growing,

present to those few neither now dumb and bedded

in a bygone week's fatigue nor abroad sodden in despair

a heavenly globe

on the hand of God

# The rains of April

In the multitudinous sheen doubled the disputatious air's

quarrel with the stone, white in black, far-flung

before my feet, mirror in liquefaction's generous hand,

tumult of year.


A tide in withdrawal from this very minute tumbling

into a guitar string's lock hold of heat: photos

of torsos, the profiles melting about the dim

pits of eyes.


Perception mirrors the eye in a gallery's

decomposition of pictures.  The window squared

cracks the pavement's recoil. Composure

is discharged.


In this artifice of the senses

multiplicity is all, the cards in the frame

above the chest of drawers, curtain drawn,

time invoked.

# TIME.

On my way to work

I walk on the evening side of the street,

The morning breaking in the breaks between the blocks

on the other side. I can no more make myself

walk up the street past the shuttered shops on the other side

than in the evening take my morning's sidewalk down.

The blandness at my left,

is always background of my motion

my energy's skateboard in the morning,

the stoop's commotion and the fire of the groceries

at night feeding helium to my emptied head

walking home sheltered on the other side.

Past habit reason, self-nurture of the engine.

with much retrieval heaves into view a station

the day that's spring

the eagle soars in eye and out of it this day

and miniscule the day impinges

its nail into the eagle's eye:


all beauty cry of what we stand to lose.

of the rain that fell briefly

earlier this afternoon only a few drops remain

each one larger than life

its past path vivid

in the distension of its shape

and their journey together

commemorated by the unequal distances between them, spray pattern

on the blue hood of a parked car.

the homeless

may sit, toes upward, faces snuggled against the stone of an edifice, so to sleep,

or on a step upright, torsos and heads in the lavish metronome nod

of the catatonic,

or in twos, fit in zigzag, knees pulled up, may lie to sleep, a single brown hand

in front of a chest rooted in the stone,

or may stand, leaning forward in the air, in confirmation of the frailty

                          of the bones about their eye

motionless, a bag on the sidewalk next to them,

or be busy, crimson about their glaring pupils, scratching, bent, their swollen

                      ankles, purple

between shoe and cuff, or lie facedown under blankets of

                    convenience

on a park bench's curving, painted slats, only their hair, copious and twisted,

                    showing, or sprawl

their face open to the sky, crucified

on the stoop of an abandoned building, but almost always their gesture

is curiously careless of their comfort,

well adapted

to the precariousness of their prospects.

Within the stoic grid

the traffic happens

subject to law

that's set in colors of flowers, leaves and sun

denied: the signals' gels proscribe

the opening: an act of intellect.

By no means will the law

submit to the indignity of nature,

by the perfect artificiality of its signals affirming itself

second nature, exemption from time.

Exposed to the law's poison, the drunk eye

rejects the comfort of chlorophyll,

petal's pride, the solace of sun, rejoicing

in the eternal motion of the traffic whipped on

by the staggered patterns

as the houses all about come and go.

neatly twisting

with a shudder of windows

into its extent's fullness,

holding it,

a beat,

slipping back into

the invisibility of

peripherality of perspective

the wild crazy hair of its fire escapes—

for just that moment the tenement embraces you

in peace of proportion

and like one of those women that are almost beautiful

just one year of their life

by a grace of brickwork tenders

the preciousness of an intimacy

barely withheld.

this giant building along whose acres  of panes
wintertime stream the people working there
by subway load down the end-lacking sidestreet
a veritable elephant among the tenements and brownstones,
inlapidate bulk, yeah, with a roof accommodating,
up to the time of the crash uptown and certain
investigations into perquisite habits
a heliport, pitifully lacks a face, subliminally horrible fact
to me who's passed it thousands of days, the vast cliff of its
                                        street front
terribly blank: as that of a man deprived of his features.
Laid in my life's path and the city's, to passing inspection
it  displays a plaque merely, from the annals of real estate crime,
                                        the janitor's
registered name.  And yet, there was a time I lifted my eyes and saw
flatly incised along the full length of its front
the name also of its owners and masters, gilt, proclaimed,
but with such cunning of discretion, my mind
could not retain it, nor
that it was there.  And this more than once.
But this morning, looking more closely I saw
a letterbox in the form, circular, of a safe's door, bronze,
and on it a seal, a merchant, his back turned to an Indian,
and behind them the sails of a ship, sheaves of wheat and corn
                                        in its leaves
in formal entwinement making some comment around them
pertaining to survival, and above the seal
a giant ferocious eagle.

the housefronts rise, windowbroken,
from side street to side street in their confusion,
each one the picture of a house, each picture
stapled to the next
above the line of shops.

if with the flourish of an animal trainer
or an explorer returned
I would point to houses
it would be the gesture of a magician's
glance conjuring
up what is not there.

and yet: what multitudes
behind these pictures!

## ABINGDON SQUARE

here, too, there is a Soldier, all in green,
his green head, face young under the doughboy hat,
shielded by the flag whose staff he is holding,
holding surprisingly a Colt in his right,
the gun, slight in the inconsonant flag's shadow,
slightly behind his back,
muzzle down from his hanging arm,
as though he were waiting, after vicissitudes down on his luck,
for his assassin in an alley in the West
that, face uplifted, he'd set out to conquer,
not soldier at all, really,
but a desperado
commemorated as soldier,
one of us,
on his rising pedestal,
among the pigeons
and the wine-sodden sleepers.

static of the cities
locked across the continent
sweltering sores in the summer's heat
in vast battle for the souls of their
festering multitudes, white and brown sons of Mary,
black children of Jesus, hummed incantation of their summer cars drifting
or rattling for fare, litany crackling
of their names from their windows' breathless
resistors, hymn of their summers
as the ritual battles are fought
by their sons, wood of the bat against desperate speed
         of the cunning ball, weary-armed, glorious,
on the greensward, moon rising, cry for the redemption
of the urbanized flesh of the poor

as with the thousand white eyes of their barrooms
the great man-eating beasts watch
crouched in the ripening acres
the shifting score
of a pre-arranged fate
desperately contested.

a hum in the air envelops the wheeling flocks of pigeons above the gliding cars,
as a newspaper page in the lesser format of the tabloids
with agility slips off the sidewalk,
and after an artistically calculated moment of hesitation
making use of the fold along its back that makes of it
two pages glides, opening and closing its wings
across the momentarily empty stage of the intersection, pausing,
the diagonal curve of its arc gracefully achieved
by the breathtaking repetition of the movement of its wings
and the ice-cool skating of plane on plane, foil frictionless,
for a tragic moment, almost crumpled, in the gutter,
in a smoothly dexterous turn, wing over wing,
never out of touch with the pavement,
ascends over the curb and is off, past the trash bin,
gaily, triumphantly,
artist aerodynamic, skilled to the point
beyond survival, as the plumb birds, yellow-eyed, faintly iridescent, erring about
                                                  on the sidewalk
jerkily peck for what crumbs I cannot imagine.

the ceremonial gravity of this bowler-hatted young man,
shuffling some distance, the white of his shirt or T-shirt clerically narrow
above his sweater
after the great big glorious ringletted whore, fat in her jeans, Sheba herself, her
hair oily,
was so great it hit my hilarity like an electrical storm and cleansed me,
restored, momentarily, my faith in human nature.

the power of her legs' columns
swinging under her skirt in the rain as she hurries
drives her effortlessly past me in the glory
of a flower of purpose nurtured
by herself in the city unaided
except by her own
kin's loving patience
through the white city

Con, dregs walking
open yes shut
from hip uneasy
looking for trouble
gets back in
fool himself.
He's fooling himself.

"Nickel," he says, "Smoke," between his teeth like at the refectory table
                                        in the big house, graduating
up to the big time, but me at the corner of 17th in the smoke of his young
business man's whisper see my old girl friend in her 35th year
slipping back into the steadying habit,
taking high aim, her nerves shot,
and the innocent enterprise of this punk
gets on my arse,
a regrettable lack of detachment.

## SATURDAY.

in summer's heat the houses boil over
into a graciousness of manners and display
from out the niches of their doorways
to the curb where on the parked cars' fenders and hoods
men sit and discourse, watching over the young women's children,
ignoring the young toughs preened for conquest, dreaming
of the 9 to 5
elusive, weaving around them
the image of the small town of their youth
on the island
when dignity was attainable
and graciousness was not sullen.

in the safe-house of my imagination slipping
through the drag net of the day to day
I have failed to notice the doctor's
total renewal of the blood, a camera I have been using lately
suddenly, instrument in my hands, and not focused on them,
revealing to me the new faces—that every summer evening an entirely new population
has come to occupy, filling the sidewalk like some beach,
the nine blocks of my daily walk, their hair strange,
a zoo, it looks like, or a circus, most distinguished gatherings
wondrously of personality, picture-costumed and with the faces of experience,
fiercely tough without inordinate din partying every evening
in the other detritus all around me, tidal wave
of poverty: in which, by no means distressed, I float, slightly uneasy, however,
at my unawareness, these ten years or more,
of a turn-over of humanity right around me, revealed to me
not by my eyes, but by a camera
turned to the sidewalk.

these faces in the doorways in the rain, grouped
with their sad mixed history, forthcoming
into the silver shade of the salsa,
perfectly characterless shell of a gaiety never felt,
for a wake for the Indian, oh sad experiment
of the Americas!

now what is one to make of the moon that rises so roundly, so fully, so
yellowly
betwixt these spires, Buddha smiling above the mountain ranges ringing
in ever expanding waves
the temple, seeing that it is so utterly an other than oneself in its
vast benignness
amidst the Art Deco above which it thrones rising, on the move, comes, going, moving,
moving?

a sullen face
a neck-alignment like a knife
an underhand look
a curved back rising from the subway

twixt curb and wall the sugared wolf pack dances
on pay day night no pay for them
they're black

## 2 A.M.

a display of shadow art works
in the mode of utmost performance mobility
is whispered across street level
every dangerous night:
it is the sky's adaptive insinuation of itself
into the pavement, ironic comment
on the solidity of our installations,
every night
exactly the same.

The
all-night
Oriental-run
fruit market and grocery
at night has this steady side-clientele
of Blacks and Hispanics lounging in the doorway next door
tonight oddly subdued
by the crewed cable-repair trucks pulled up by the curb
the hard-hats in their leisurely manner steadily doing the work
they get paid for, enviably
holding down their jobs.

One imagines because of all the light sources at different heights
and of different intensities, each reaching out into the
                              space of the street
with an imperial hand though sometimes feeble,
that the air is full of complex shadows, in three dimensions extending
                              within it, dark bodies, whereas,
there is in this  2 a.m. space of the street only the uniform night
                              equitably
stretching from beyond the by no means visible stars
and reaching down in between the houses, but, though in and of itself
                              a uniform darkness,
not unlike that of a material world generally, to different degrees
                              and in
different manners variously between the houses occupied by the reaching
                              bodies of light of those manifold glowing
or radiant sources, overlapping, touching and fusing, struggling
                              up from the pavement, the
bodies of gladiators grappling, composite angels in the world's darkness,
perceived as the shifting shadow of the city night at its clear-ringing
                              apex
at which dies the previous day's life with a shout of desperate joy
(before onset of the night's deeper second half), a shifting shadow
                              in whose movement
a cry for help must needs go unheeded, unlocalizable in the
                              light-cancered broken
space between the houses, seeming to the home-going motorist an
                              illusion
in this illusory movement of illusory shadow in the air
                              at this late and not yet early hour.

the clanking end of night, unquiet night,
the mind's disturbance before dawn
when paranoia squats upon the fender in guise of laughing girl
and eye is shadow-given to glowing license plates
from out of state.  On which, it's true, the tincture of the day, to-morrow,
                                        infuses,
but does not yet offend the madness of the stage, its blackness, its quality
                                        of nest, its nearness,
its screaming flow of light.  Surprises me.

Caught by my hurry I descend
a half hour before dawn.

silently at night the city sheds its image of stone
emerges naked, sheer shadow, mounts softly
swelling about the players' backs

silently at night the city sheds its image of stone
emerges naked, sheer shadow, mounts softly
swelling the players, its dream muscled,
the space of a darkness, for a cool spasm,
mere dream

silently at night the city sheds its image of stone
emerges naked, sheer shadow, mounts softly
washes the dreamers, out walking,
of purpose, lethal

The three ladies
hoarsely enjoy
their cigarettes together
before turning in,
one on the sidewalk,
one on the steps,
and one up by the door
to the Allerton Hotel
in the doorway's light
half a block from the corner,
at 4 a.m. on Memorial Day Weekend, a Sunday
1985.

Walking to work the strong lights give me a multiplicity of shadows
forever overtaking me, growing strong as they catch up with me and only gradually
                                        fading
having done so and running ahead though none of them lasting
from one light to the next, but each one frightening me in turn as darkening
                                    energetically
it winds its way up from behind me, replica of the young murderers whose loosely
                                smiling faces over their beer cans
make my knees weak in retrospect as I walk to work
of the value of which, non-committally , I am not convinced, hereof happy, guarded
from the evidence of its nearly utter insignificance, off the side-walk, upright,
                                    striding,
effectively without a shadow of my own.

The street unfolds not equilateral, a gaming board against a wall of life,
in cunning varied with the sun, the river's bride at elbow's end,
aurora of the shops my hollow shield at evening time, lifegiving rich,
the stone as desert there as naught for me to caravan across the other time.

This is the given of a pendulum that swings in arcs by hairs decreased
from bed and board to thieving den, the place in which my brain is bled,
a rod of brass suspended from the air unheld, my swing beneath the apple tree,
as in the semblance of a man I vent my dulling gleam.

The sidewalk is my place.  I marvel at its history, the filigree of giants' work,
                              a garden at my feet.
The storm of windows musical, aurora's gift, benumbs my brain.
In gratitude I savor the shops of summer and winter's rowdy party nights
as in a one-way traffic unrelenting my dominoes are placed.

He negotiates the entrance to the grocery, all jelly within his clean clothes,
                                        with great delicacy.  He is solving the
                                        problem
of reconciling verticality with forward motion having had to face the fact
                                        that man can't slide
but must advance by steps, in progressive bifurcation.
A lifetime diet of alcohol has resolved him into pure consciousness.

She stands on that same corner every morning.
I could describe her particular dress but the point is
her outline is neat, almost an oval, and there are touches
of color.  She stands there every morning.

The street's look
drifts through her eyes.
They look at one another,
we see one another,
don't look as we pass.  She's a crazy woman,
no need to embarrass her.  I respect her for
being so neat, for her regular habits, and for holding herself so straight.
                              My values stand out in all kinds
of weather, the southwest corner of 20th.
But with summer coming on, I have been looking at her more
                              closely,
her purse, her fold-up umbrella, and made the discovery, taking the advantage,
                              of looking at her in profile,
she standing there like the widow at the sea shore,
that her lips are shaking, her flaw as image, and was shocked, aggrieved on
                              her behalf, and on my own,
at her flaw: so self-contained in her outline, engaged in a perpetual coming apart
at her center, a mouth in commotion, and if I had more time for ceremony
or could weep, I would have wept for her, that is, it would have been the
                              occasion for that: to go aside and sit and weep.
This morning I looked at her for the first time, met her eyes and seeing a
                              movement on her face, smiled
the ready stiff small smile one has ready, and her face distracted into a
                              grimace.
Now I don't know if she was showing ironic contempt for my inability to

maintain non-recognition, mocking
me with some slight savagery, or if the rictus within which her eyes flared
was a genuine smile, better than mine, but distorted by some muscular
                                    dyscontrol
akin to a fluttering of her lips, the warfare in the flesh of her
                              face
a heroic containment which her self-exhibition on that corner every morning,
                              all in hand, perfectly still image,
represented.

Fearful to meet one's emblem.

I see the same grey-haired man
patrolling the grates, head down, shambling,
his feet heavy, a little, on the sidewalk between their stretch
up to Harlem.  Sharp-eyed he must be to see the coin
chance has fumbled for him.

Indeed, if in a dream, space shifting in rags as though all places
indefinitely themselves only, unlocated, seems superior to time ordered
in its three-pronged fork, unilinear from bracketed moment to next,
by its liberty of displacement, the bunch of footholds, precisely, of your unown
                              dream, befittingly disquieting,
the morning's seam throwing the dream's transtemporal fluidity into a city
                              street's straight line, eerily dissolves
the night's phantom solidity of matter
into aspect of time, and it is now along this straight line of space that you
                              wander inmidst the dance of time, firework
of moments a jump about one another in the dress of hueing, of sonorities, of
                              odors
and of pedestrians in contrary motion, disjointed and disordered: only
day sorts them both out.

The shift from grey to yellow, black, emergence of the strong color, its recession,
the waxing and waning, the reorganization of sound, accelerations and slowings,
are not epiphanies of matter, the bane, but of time, the nemesis, geared to its
gears,
the clock going round and round, unspooling, immaterial in the city's myriad
minds,
the hecatomb of lives diffusing in performance, wearing out purposely
against matter, structure of the field of action.

There is a certain association between darkness and coldness.
Though colder, the patches of shade in the side street
                    seem like the warming snow drifts
that the spent traveler dies in.  But those that through their fault or not
                    have to sleep in the streets
seem to prefer the sunnier spots at night, fine-grained by the street lights,
an avoidance of the victimizers by their
                    victims.  When morning comes
everybody is up and about.  To me these mornings, coming from a warm bed, showered,
                    seem especially cold, the sun's warmth in winter
an illusion. Yet by their waking motion these unfortunates or guilty ones
                    seem
to endorse the sun's warmth in the city street on a morning in which I shiver.
Perhaps they fit dark sleep to the darkness of night, as though an owl's child
nesting close to its parent, curled up for darkness, fleeing nothing, seeking
                    darkness.  But why would not these dark ones seek rather
                    to flee the day?
Yet, when I am up early, before dawn, hurrying through the winter night's ending,
to me the night's darkness is indistinguishable from its cold, the cold, to me,
                    stepping forth in selfhood with the light of morning,
a sheet glass through which to walk,
sparkling in its ascent to the heavens in the eerie rays of an unwarming sun,
memento of ice in its translucency.  What warms these illuminaries may be their
                    visibility to others, each day
a reprieve into humanity's perhaps not altogether illusory, through slight
brotherhood.  Are they colder in the day or at night?
It may to them be an academic question.  The intricacies of another man's struggle
                    for survival
tend to escape one.

### JAN. 3RD.

in the tremendous roar of 8 o'clock,
the turning over of a new leaf,
the copper windows shine
(now that it it's winter and the sun is low).
through the streets the fuckers move
as though humanity incarnate
in a giant animal of steel
leaping uptown.

Walking to work.

I meet them.
More and more their faces are familiar.
Clad in their coats and gait.
We meet in passing.
Upright all as yet.
But if any one of them I did not see any more, I could not miss them.
Approaching in a meeting that is a recession behind my back my wonderment is not
                                                    of them but of their recognition of me.
In them I'm there.
And each time as though we were such unheavenly bodies as would never meet anymore.

In the sadness of cars two or three years old and already worn out
all these cars the faces communing,
equal in the rushing morning hour
their sadness slowly speeding through the ever rebuilt houses
and houses ever so many shifting all about, a world,
the bodies thinking waiting for the light to change, heads slumped
above the inert wheel
show the grid's shuttle of unused time
in the clear light of grainy sadness.

A kind of politeness dominates the street here
in these parts of town where an excess of color equates with poverty
inasmuch as the obstructive lingering in groups
and the aggressive straight walk
are the acknowledgements that the other is there, is
one's judge over whom one must prevail
in which hierarchies, those also of school yard and jail corridor, instantly form, reform.
The pecking order of the times when domestic fowl ran free,
the street being the place of habitation, apartment mere temporary withdrawal, cool
off the yard.

He mentioned to his companion his starship
as I passed them, walking down the avenue,
in an off-hand manner, not a rich man, depressed,
like it might have been his dog,
a pedestrian in the shadow of television.

Their gladrags are picking up power this spring,
more compactly assorted, a fashion's aggression having gone out of them,
multi-layered cocoon from which emerges
the butterfly of their mind, glory-winged
picture of a grasp on oneself
in the gender language of found retail outlets
                              neither boutique nor second hand stores,
a serious undertaking this spring,
which makes me breathe easier
as the decade breaks.

It is undoubtedly an American,
but a gross sight, he is defecating in the doorway,
his pants down decently in the back only,
in a crouch, ready to jump, peering about apprehensively,
his large face up and moving.

The jetsam floats immersed in air upon the pavement
in utter desperation down the Sunday morning
caught in the anguish of its truth.

The lobsters are dead in this tank.  Above the bank of carapaces
red and black a few antennae wave.
The tank sits sleazy in the light of Sunday morning.
It is a case of murder by neglect.  For the death glorious of the
                                            animal
thrown struggling into the boiling water
for transformation to a feast has been substituted
a suffocation in the night, the end as garbage.
The chain of life is broken.

The three faggot queens emerge from their transvestite night of self-sale
(individually sauntering their long slim brown legs displayed
along the line of traffic) having, their morning cup of coffee,
divested themselves of their miniskirts and elegance of blouses
in some ducked-into two-family brownstone basement entrance,
and now stand, in mock independence united, a short line, all three
                                        hailing for cabs
in the morning traffic uptown, their arms elegantly curving the mock-disdain in
                                        the air, all dressed in white, and male:

a cab stops finally and they converge upon it, requesting, seated,
their gay little party be brought uptown
to the sweltering mazes of Harlem,
thus working in their minimum rebellion and quest for a living
a small con on the white cabbie, the Magi,
hitching a ride in the desert.

Of late, more and more often, in the street men carry
the faces of Indians as though some upheaval
had brought to the fore in their faces the arched cheekbones, opaque
agate eyes, the wide expanses on skulls like boulders
of this race exterminated hereabouts and in the islands, the cast
of features of these victims, integrity of impassive non-collaboration,
pressing forward in these aliens
shaped, I surmise,
not by blood but by circumstance.

I of late observe the sparrows too trusting
tardying in the soundwaves of my descending soles
or perhaps their wits sickened by the standard of emissions
in the city's great sundriven alembic of air
so that to their decaying brains the kingdom of god peaceable seems
at hand about them on the pavement.  I would rather have them flee from me,
the monster of nature, man.

Would you put yourself at the viewpoint of this overly painted woman
you can easily do so overtaking her, walking a little slowly two
                                        steps ahead and to the side, observing
the looks of the men coming onto her,
her point of view.

CITY.

every stone here seems in some way precious
for having the genuineness gone in the cement

not so for the greenery, artifact growing
in the cracks

nor for the margin littoral of the sky, pale aviary
in the corner of the eye of the pedestrian

but most satisfying of all are the windows,
convict eyes cleansed of the rot of reminiscence.

The day explodes and suddenly the air is full of people
the sack of night so sudden they tumble fresh bathed
in the latex of their rendition, the world at hand, communists
of the pavement, unready
as though there were a god.

The pedestrian hides within the darkness of his dress his predilections,
tracemarks
like the fine rifts in the stones of some inspiration infused in him
in the days of his childhood by some comic book or by the challenge
of the only society he will ever know, the kids in his high school class
or by some sudden vision in some sweater or cap, affordable
of a gesture toward life, revealing his artistry through the veil of
his uniform
only to the additional quarter second of the regard: in the abortion of his
desire
standing forth as an individual, viz. a vision of an identity mythical
contained
in the extra width of a cuff, or the excessive length of a tight skirt, or in
some faint principle of contrast
between hue of blouse and jacket, or the adumbration of an abstract figure
in the cast from shoulder to hip, or in some weird outfit altogether, a
revolutionary gesture
into which the rebellion of his adolescence has congealed, fashion of the ghetto.
The dark and ill-dressed crowd only a hair's breadth from a ragged rabble
in a switch of the eye's wavelength resolves
into a costume ball of the utmost refinement.

If all about, the stone rises
festooned by sunshine's retail commerce of color at its lower edges,
it is in celebration of an event antedating the advent
of this hastening crowd milling
in illusory rectitude darkly in the sunshine,
the invention of a geometry
to which the course of life could be aligned, disciplined
by the illusion of Euclid that never
ever the twin lines of their advent would meet.

He comes out of the side street glowering he is black
as he sees me looking that way but I was only
it is barely April looking at the at this time
all over this lower westside's gentrified sidestreets flowering
white-blooming tree-sized blooms' globes in a promising white shot through
                              with a gray, charmingly tentative,
in a vista rising above his dark person, clutching some object
though not the usual bottle in a brown bag.
We repeat this dialogue, our paths having nearly crossed a moment later
across the street keeping moving in our diverse directions.
Oh innocence oh guilt
oh life oh spirit
we all some three score years do as best we can.

The workmen's hefty swagger about their tight hips
as they sip their styrofoam coffee
carries the soaring structure's coup.
Their tremor betrays them.
They will be out of here in no time,
voters for the wrong candidate.

She walks clutching her dog's shit
bent over painfully.  I turn to see if her legs
are thin and hard-lined as I think, if
her dress or coat is awry as I suspect, that of a madwoman,
or of someone distraught, but her dog, dancing gaily, turns too, so that I look
                                    quickly
toward a man passing on the other side of the street  looking for the dog
this one by his attention favored, expecting to see her, prancing also, or
                                    peeing, or standing
indifferently, but seeing no other animal whatsoever on this early morning street
                                    realize
I was the one my passing friend favored.
I draw the line at fucking dogs.  Fucking dogs, to my mind,
is a filthy, disgusting habit.

The giant crullers, glazed Danish, succulent
doughnuts, all
just a shade larger than you would have thought possible, as though sprung
from some special seed cultivated in a sixth borough beyond the Bronx explode
in my side as in the early morning I walk past, feeling better.

Teach walks to work, unnaturally straight,
                              his briefcase stuffed.
His expression is not unkindly
but it is infinitely too much painfully preoccupied
by himself for his profession: his life
is too hard.
For those he teaches, short-changed,
and for himself.

The airbrakes' hiss ascending
through the grill's meticulous iron pattern
release and stop, long, short,
you are reassured: things
are being taken care of.

These women are dressed nice and these men
wear clean clothes walking to work
between 7 and eight, they are
celebrants with the others
of the rites of meeting in defiance of circumstance, to wit,
the hardness of life.

The light lies flat on the posters
alchemically raising from them a great whiteness
a hidden treasure briefly allowed them to offer to us
in hands lent to them by the light
proudly, lifted out and up from under
the grime covering them of printed faces, shrugged off.
Light is the tantalizer, and there is no reason, really, not to call it "god,"
                                    unless it be

this word's darkness.

It's beginning to get hot in the early morning.
The great beast
crawling forward toward you
under the shade of the avenue ahead is summer.

They are kidding one another
in the interval before work.
The topics are dangerous.  This is an operation
light and easy, continuous accompaniment
of cooperation in work, an indispensable cleansing
of the atmosphere breathed by them jointly,
a pleasure to accomplish, a hair's breadth, really
away from Hobbes' war, what makes it worthwhile
to come to work, the civility of insult, yet also
perpetuation of certain ancient hierarchies, almost imperceptible, not least
of race, in a shifting balance of forces, registered
in the same language, by banter, the war
domesticated, the hardness of life
transmuted
partially.

In the new morning I receive the street's bouquet.
I notice, my face thrust into the light's fragrance,
the houses, packed, regarding me as though, empty of life, wondering
whereto would their accolade serve me, would I,
my skin oily with the flower of day, simply inebriate be, ingratiate
                           supping
on the city's flesh, withholding my own, or,
the sun's pollen gilding the dark crevices of my cortex, return
the favor, unfold, & flower, bright-hued, on the long sidewalk,
or make my obeisance by a gift of lightness, or by, perchance, better,
a turn in my work, reflecting, circuitously, almost impossibly,
through those blind windows welcoming me.

He is clearly though not at this moment, hands up, calmly
looking around, gesticulating, talking to one person or almost while
                              being with another, all in a nothing place
                              on the curb,
a liar, the which to tell by his eyes' largeness, posed on his cheek bones
way out front, compact opaque disks supported
by a smoothly functioning swiveling system underneath at the moment in low gear,
                              confrontational organs so mendacious
they seem black and the pupil inside white, impression carried away.
But how he gave himself away even to a glance lasting surely a period of time
                              less than or at most a fifth of a second
                              was his relaxed face, relieved
that at the moment there was no reason for lying, not even an occasion for it,
                              the face didn't have to work
supporting those two globes' intense overwhelming of another gulping them up
                              in a spreading embrace simulating transparency,
a hard labor using up the man from which this no-man was momentarily absolved, but
                              even so, ineluctably, his eyes bore witness to him
so that I carried away nothing
but those two misused eyes.

I have seen both of them often.  The one just an old man, one of those,
                              perhaps Irish,
wary-looking, with that air of secrecy of the Irish about him,
long and thin, the set of his moving body intimating the alcoholic, but never
drunk; not a bum; just a local resident; the other a character,
always on the street, leaning, invariably, on a parking meter in an extremely
                              comfortable posture,
seeming the observer of the street life yet never seeming to look
and as soon as the weather is warm enough taking his shirt off, getting a tan,
                         the street his beach, why not: apparently having
                         nothing ever to do,
and in this way a man of leisure, but his queer demeanor and his pockmarked, bulbous-
                         nosed face and his inert eyes
giving him the appearance of dumbness and even derangement, of a madman,
but this morning I saw #1 passing this one, hardly stopping, slip him the like of
                         a dollar bill, mumbling something,
the other, unchanged, wordless, pocketing the bill without concern.
I first thought: a case of panhandling but then remember I'd seen him dozens of
                         times sunning himself, his folded skin for all to see,
and never addressing a word to anyone, and in sum the dignified one, asking nothing
                         of nobody, like a statue in a fountain,
so thought, by God! a numbers runner or taking the bets on the track,
and though this may not be true, admired this life of passive hiding in exposure,
                         all dignity maintained and no lie spoken,
and the sharpness of mind of a man taking the bets,
never taking notes, and not minding
seeming dumb,
even crazy.

When the darkness wears thin in the air, substance almost leached out,
but is still the world's temporal definition making it
the box of night, time has stretched
for those up and about since the evening
almost to the breaking point
and in the tensions of their scarce scatter
frayed in the fomentation of their weariness
the time of exaltation has come
to block with a wall of blinding glare
the unfaceable advent of  return to habitation
by the quick execution of a crime.
But alas! In this superb hour the tide of night, mistress of the heart,
invisible, is rushing out through the innumerable small side streets' leaks
and nothing is done.
The statistics show the peak of crime some hours earlier
in the merry center of darkness.
Man is weak.
Yet in the register of his excellence, his emotion,
it is the hour before dawn that is the apex.

I have repeatedly noticed, not being struck by them, the inordinate profusion
of small and even tiny, tea-colored organic shapes accumulated
in an almost lively manner as a small seam along the curbs, annual sedimentation
of  the sexual organs of trees, persisting in their country fashion, so it seems,
through winter, a residue figuring, though presumably inert, the hope of the
                                        living
for a fortunate encounter that might yet occur, but until this instant the thought
that  in view of the radical impermanency of gross artifact trash on the street,
                            ever new,
this brown near-dust, clinging to the sheltering curb demonstrated life's extraordinary
                            force
had not occurred to me.

her face was so ambiguous in its morningside inwardness's confusions
I turned to see her figure and was struck to perceive a like turmoil
                              at her ankles,
the inordinately long coat mixing there in the context of an encounter with the socks
                              she had not straightened out
with an equally inexplicably long white coat of the sort doctors or nurses wear
but coming down almost to her feet and sticking out, partly, underneath her
                              overcoat,
so that going to her boss's office or other place of employment
she was probably mulling over the current intertwining of the strains
                              of a frank but unresolved personality
invested by her in the care of people, and probably to their advantage,
considering the altogether inordinate length of the outer garments loosely
                              hanging over, not really covering,
her person, which was on the small side.

A tender groove, clemently gentle in shallowness, its grey
blue immixture of rain and straight-fired metal
a running lying from a there to a there unmarked by notches
of a beginning and an end section longitudinal
of what is thought of as a conduit is all of an intrusion, image floating
in some days' haze or other in support of an inattention
to the street I walk on, intimating
the rainwash in the arroyo secco, star-fixed from the mountains,
collapse of bridges, the flow of the tributary
unimpeded; or the toy-like suspension
of a once-drawn line in a sketch
that one need not look at.

the silver of their rearview mirrors' fat globs
glinting in their faces of conspirators
silently as in a storm of chirping birds they slide
curbside sanctifying
blood's spring in day's turning,
with their darkness all
in containment.

the supermacho faggot drifts
shifting but slow his mask to daylight
in the still water white of dawn
his yet tough skin holding within
the calm theatre of bygone night: I regret
a curious look not locking
making flick too fast his face
back one more time to fit
into the turmoiled dream of day softened to the hardness
of an everyday life,
just another
middle-aged man.

The snow lines the tree above this Irish drunkard
youthfully old in his decay, as they always are
wound around the tree's trunk at 5 in the morning
still in his "sir" and "please" and "insolence"
carrier of the tradition of '48, year of the potato famine
and of the seaboard slums from New York to Albany and over to Boston
of the Irish, charming men who had given up and whorish drunken women
carrying over from the last century into this,
up through the wave of a new underclass, Negro,
what professors have called a culture of poverty,
for every two blacks, drunks, derelicts, beggars, bums on this street
one still Celt, or perhaps one per three or four, filthy,
sleeping in doorways in couples, oddly the sharpness of mind,
a cunning pointed or weak, upthrusting through the mud of their minds,
some observation useful to a beggar, and some admirable disdain,
the loser's knowledge that makes him noble.

At odd hours of the pavement individuals appear
at 5 a.m. this 2 p.m. man midtown by his attaché case downtown
or perhaps what looks like a returned sailor off the docks
except for the halt in his gait having no place to go
a woman at that dangerous age of thirty, respectable, her eyes emboldened
by her lifetime's time at an hour when the straight look is dangerous.

## A WALK NOT QUITE A STROLL.

a turbulence if truth be told
at the intersection of the planes of experience and objecthood
street intersection in slow rotary motion up perhaps
30° from the horizontal, its cross rotating
through my vision
in the markings of a manhole cover: pavement squares and rectangular
                              front frames
of houses clockwise, but with the white of my eyes
steady in my forward motion I know the street to be as it IS, steady
all the windows in place
as I and it pursue the same path
into a flickering Now, the moment
in the inward vision of a preoccupation by some constellation: appearing,
not quite, in the black and white of a photograph grossly
                              enlarged, the
epileptic's vision, throat-tight, but point
disappearing
in the linear segment it takes me to get from the house to
                              the office,
sixteen minutes maybe, somehow:  turbulence of my ordering mind hovering
                              roof high
above my body rolling in the circular motion of my legs linearly down one
side of a street between absolutely still linearly aligned block fronts
                              of houses, the
pilot: the turbulence of an incessant ordering intangible of what,
                              however
is itself a worse turbulence, the turbulence of my actual life,
                              experience,
the carousel of the world about me sucked into the vortext of my inner eye
incessantly, as to all outward appearance calmly
I get my arse to work.  Yet, what if the world itself
were but the edge of a turbulence?

the purr of a hood
or a small cloud of noise sound carried ahead of the car's
body, soft brush sound of plastic, now and then
an engine, far gone or in need of a tuning
in the faint percussion of a ticking or rattle,
and altogether nighttime traffic, perhaps especially so on gay early-summer
Saturday night (girls going home from the highschool dance) to Sunday morning
is different from the dense-pack swarming of even a low-density day's traffic.

But what the cars sound like
is different from what they give you to hear
coming up on you passing, passing away
or starting up, speeding up, moving, slowing down, stopping, the ear's two
patterns of the traffic's movement past and of the movement's movement merging
in the diastole pitch of breath.  Unless you lay
your ear into sound space, where hum thickens into buzz and the buzz unfolds
into not quite music but
almost like animal speech, or leaf-speak.

splendidly the barbarians crowd up, a state-subsidized
tenement, miniatures framed
in the checkered canyons beyond the doorway,
file in a spinning out of time  along the sidewalk,
in couples and triads in their choice costumes
sauntering toward us, in ceremonials if greeting merging, clustering
in mutual address, or bent on spurious errands,
on their heads displaying faces
arranged in the modes of dignity and open privacy
exempt from the demeaning stamp of responsibility.

# MARCH '91

It's winter, though on some days it seems not so.  The war is scarcely
                              finished but spirit quickly moves: a poster
fairly printed in black on white evokes the crimes committed, ours.

The stooping figure, seemingly disdainful, centered in the vast confusion
of the spreading trash.  His arms encumbered.  I, passing, fatherlike
but he was not so young, admonished him, a citizen's remark, but was embarrassed
as abruptly, birdlike, he jerked himself away, snapped out of it, head bent, with
                                        no rejoinder
acknowledging authority, took off, walked rapidly away.  Put in my place
I walked away, continuing, humiliated truly.  His madness true was cunning.

I notice that these non-poems deal more and more with derelicts that
                              cling to Manhattan
but don't have an apartment.  It is possible that these people
so like the savage of 18th century Baja California
whose souls the Jesuit fathers saved expediting their passage hence
                              simultaneously, saintly
murderers, have as the newspapers make it their business to proclaim
                              incessantly
greatly augmented in number in number since I first walked this street.  It is also
                              possible, however,
that some change in me has made it impossible for me to focus
on my avenue's inanimate artifact.

that the street at night is part of the night
is true, and that it is part of the city,
it is out of the world and people are in it,
it does not belong to them, nor is it of theirs,
so, flayed, at night, the street is another world
and all the preparations notwithstanding is quite other than what we call
                              "during the day,"
and so is most appropriate to the young not of this world
and to the old out of it, and is a savage place and restful
its penniless projects of murder and the many enterprises of suicide
wakingness' benign shadow, substance replacing matter
as in the dreams in beds in rooms color secludes the sleepers
                              each corner
by two strings connected with the moon and its attendant white star.
so of the city as a thing of the night is the street.  An equation surprising,
                              as the roar swells in the morning
though simple evidence to the walker at night: the work of man built out of
                              shadow substantial, the opposite of light,
convent maze.

that the street at night is part of the night
is true and also that though it is part of the city
it is out of the world and does not belong
to the people in it but these are on their own, nearly broke
and savage, flayed
of their ballroom diamonds down to murderer
in the street's white gash, real
in the street's soft shadow of stone.

The house was unique.  Teeming with tenantry, dark, rough
poor from the Island, on bad days lurking in its doorways, on good
socializing on the narrow sidewalk, it was a block long: but graceful.
Some builder had achieved this miracle upon himself, a tenement
ornamented richly but with balance of the medallions, the three
cornices holding the vast house together above its innumerable windows,
slight suitable horizontals maintaining the fine brick of the façade: here and there
one of these quasi-sculpted heads indistinctly recalling Tragedy and Comedy,
                              in the rectangle's pattern, regularly,
Neptune or Minerva, some long ago advertisement for hair oil: all with the
                              extreme modesty, of course, of industry
                              and within the necessary confines
of a reasonable profit on the rent, perhaps even a more than reasonable one,
and still and all and yet not depriving passer-by or tenant of all inspiring grace.  But
city ordinance holds the landlord liable for falling masonry, and faced with
                              the choice of suitable repairs
and of a simple removal of the cornices, the present owners removed them,
in March of 1987, above the five stories
with a grotesque crown of yellow concrete: so that now
the house hurts one's heart, makes one's spirit sink, shocks one, every morning
                              hollows one out, its tenants housed now
in subsistence.

They took out this house, the whole
block.  It disappeared.
Behind their huge white skeletal hands
moving as a fog.  And left a fence, solid,
board to board, continuous, lilac shading to violet, demarcating
the empty lot, that somebody wrote on
 in the beautiful lettering of graffiti, quoting Lorca,
"they kill people in New York City." The writers are unknown,
unknown also
those that left.  As the city moves,
only the huge mass of the poor
remains to itself equal.

As vehicles like jewels, set into dying night, I might mention
this ten-year old model, its noise
all the rattle of its undercarriage, intact,
but in one's mind's eyes pitted
by a soft looseness of the muffler,
prowling loosely in a slippery path

the compact closed van barreling, not very fast,
across the avenue, its white side black
full-bodied
running canvas

a traditional garbage truck,
the whine of its low-driving gears
wrapped about its engine

this seeming hotdog and chestnut cart, broken mast prone,
trundled up the avenue
in a play of buddies all screams,

the old car
figuring crime, the dementia of the prowler from Jersey, its raging mind subtly
revealing itself in a sustained rattle.

The flamboyance of the others is merely entertainment, the death of night
as feast of the epiphany.

That something perfectly false should come up
is always in the cards of the sea-swell not
this greyness, wet water and then the sand under the sea-kelp, foam to jelly,
but the mermaid, a rearing-up centerfold suggestive
of the word "loveliness," the cask of doubloons beached.  Oh
how long we were becalmed in those iridescent waters of absolute golden calm
                                        mystery of the night: so also
some apparition on the dawn street rigged by the cancerous brain of advertising men
decked out in purple and insignia of yester-year before all was lost
or even something a garbage man dreamed up in a perfect fury of film-making.

The street is not dull, its dullness not just the tense net of crime all about one,
                            tentacular time,
this being a mere though interesting aspect of
                            these rigged spectacles,
the shiver of emptiness, blur intrinsic of location: in a hail of arrows you walk
transpierced every morning so that like a sieve you sit down into work you
can't recall, the newspaper vendor's curve momentarily laced with
                            leisure
against the closed canvas of his boutique.

High rents notwithstanding
a man may still find a shop
in whose window he can indulge in a display of his nature
insidiously inserting into the purport of a sales effort
evidence of his perversion.

The brown of the houses, mute attendants, an aging of the red and the black,
                              unemphatic in the now following
a goodly number—a single white-painted wooden house, home around the corner to a
                              liquor dealer, its boards narrowly overlapping—
is the wrap trailing in the shadow hardness of asphalt and concrete that figures the
                              land.  This my route is at its heart old country, a
                              reject, quietly victorious.  The land
is not black but is black. These all are no colors: color is absent, but neither black
                              and white, photography's seeming  alternative.  It
                              is just that unviewed even as seen an indeterminacy
in this regard is the eye's compact.
The multiplicity of colors accorded to words is a mere sprinkling instantly sunk into
                              stone.
However, I have left out the people.  Here the urge of flower asserts itself.  I see
                              the African lore of  queendom,
black and yellow, the dun rose petal of a mature housewife, the vivid diagrams of
                              green, yellow and red on street jackets in fashion.
But the striking phenomenon is the street's refusal to choose between color and
                              black and white, an assertion of function and form,
                              of

mere existence.

I frequently hear people screaming in the streets.
There is in this an arrest of the traffic.
Some of them move along, turning perhaps frequently as though leaving the scene
of a fight.  These are screams of anger given the form of righteous indignation.
In their faces I see shamefaced marginality like an oily sheen, a consciousness
                                perhaps
of the occasions missed for speaking up.  One I saw this morning, a white boy,
                        had stopped in front of the local
                        5-film cinema's closed broad glass doors
and faced himself in bodily composure venting unintelligibly:  I had been wondering
why unlike the others he did not seem to be parliamenting down an invisible interlocutor,
but then surmised he could see his reflection in the bland dark doors.
I am uneasy with the sheer prose quality of the last two lines and the cheapness of my
                                attempt
to redeem it by "bland dark doors" and wonder if these dualist soliloquizers likewise
criticize their forensics somewhere behind their twisted faces, their argument ascending
                        through the traffic like smoke
darkly upward to the choir white, attempt futile for the books.


Everybody wants to be saved on their own terms.  But what is rhythm?  The redemption of
error by error: art.

A break stop would stop the eye were it not focused on the
foothold, an open spot, white, toward which flash the parked cars, flashes
the flight of parked cars into which is inset an eye, my eye.  I am moving alright.  This
empty area even so on the temporal micro-sale is alike to a major calamity, a dead
sea yet also only an impression that I might not have on any other day,
a veritable nothing.  I could adduce innumerable facts about this street corner, crossing
of corners, histories of each corner thereon,  the gone doughnut shop, the gone second
                                        floor
Korean bordello above it (now a billiard hall), the savings bank that went broke
paying 5 1/2 rather than 5 percent, was sold to an uptown bank, then closed for good
its fat honeybees still swarming, a certain niche harboring a certain homeless person
                                        two winters in a row, Slater's with George's tiny
ballpoints, etc.

The rush of the still cars as I slowly gain on them is a delusion, a
metaphor, my mind walks so much faster in the morning or for time and of a perspective
                                        though it is like a flight of birds
migrating.  I don't see (feel) it in the evening no doubt because I am then walking opposite
to the cars' pointing.  As for the break intercutting it it is but a change of
                                        direction.
Why I talk I don't know.  I continually discover my own unwinding mendacity, exempla
gratia the calamity above alleged of 8th and 14th when in truth it is a hardly perceived
                                        nothing on a singular hence insignificant
occasion, mere illustration of the TRUTH that absent focus anything is truly nothing.
Exemplifying Stein's dictum the void self is continually engaged in a mission of
                                        gathering importance by larcenous
fabrication.  The meters have expired always.  So rarely as to be never have I seen anybody
park their car or family-wise get in through its opened door and arc it away.

It was a pleasant morning.  I noticed the augmented activity of the birds
who went to the length of sitting in the small bare trees as though by their bombastic
                                        chests
they could give a preview of leafage.
The man at the corner I noticed really all winter a fixture in the wall, seated each
morning in a shallow niche as though too big for the shrine
inert and at most whispering as I passed could I spare a dime
was up and walking in his multi-colored togs agitatedly speaking with teeth
like thick white spittle about "something to eat".
He didn't spoil the coming of spring for me between Palm Sunday and Easter
but rather seemed himself in his awkward human way
another figuration of its explosion through the dawn, the air achirp
and this demented man too numb normally even to beg
flinging his teeth into the air angry for a bite
at the end, this time around, of many cold nights in a wall.  Nevertheless the conjunction
of agitations struck at me, cast doubt, in retrospect, on the bona fides of a pigeon
I had encountered earlier about my feet on the sidewalk
with an excessive confidence not breaking its stride for me.

The vast truck turns onto the avenue with such a stately turn
on it only, lashed, three big heavy boxes like lead batteries
its tail almost bending with deference toward its sleek precious load so that
in all male faces at this pre-business dawn hour there appears
marginally the age-old male face of the expert esteeming nothing so much
as a good set of tools or a job well-handled though most of us here
                                        are ignorant bums of course
because the load was heavy but simple though no one could tell what it was,
showing the truth, the simplicity everlasting of real industry
far from the hype of the computer and videoscreens and busily idle salesmen
the "megabytes," the "microchips," the hype of complexity trying to sell us
this putrescent civilization as though corporate industry by some
                                        spirituality of its workings
approached the dead God's comprehensive fullness of mind: a heavy load
swinging slowly around a corner
on an enormous flatbed trailer
in the white morning,
like a black snake.

# c. 1990, A.D

the savagery of faces in the street
florescent circus of the Island and Uptown
has now sombered into the Imperial City's exposition of the Universal Proletariat.
Within the canopy of traffic the more natural hue of the sun-adapted epidermis
is now foundation only
of the masks dancing of a humanity diversifying around the globe.
A nobility of identity has taken hold, awesome glare
of the struggle for survival
within the densening crowd.

It is not often that one sees the face of malice yet sometimes the bully's smile
the contemplation inward ravished of some hurt to be inflicted
or that slyly he got away with
just recently,
a haughty closure of the nurse's face, the nurse's sadist distance
that feeds on victims with disdain: her gloating secret.

The street's pedestrians are thinking in the mornings
and wreathed in darkness daydream the drivers at the stop lights dream
of what contents them,
bear witness to the inward motion of stationary thought
the dream boat of pedestrians ahead of time
the driver's silent motor idling at the stop light
each man alone with what contents him.

the man's curved back
he is leaning back
he is sitting on a bar stool
this is breakfast time but not quite yet
the man's curved back, a soft line down his front, is held
by a beginning gesture of her arm across the counter, white and elbow
or
some general disposition of a uniformed waitress
                              between coffee urn and the
matitudinal customer: now it seems to me I see a blaze of light between these two
people sheer and white
arrived bouncing off a piece of cutlery and the white walls
but flaring up there
in a benign obliteration of detail
and as though circumstance served it
consuming itself in a blaze of ephemeral intelligence
never detail, all circumstance
and sort of maybe even happy about it
not that it made me feel good
but I am grateful for it
so regrettably circumstantial to myself
unfeeling pedestrian (traveler)
intelligence

On these walks this season, returned, though I  did not miss what next to me, passed,
was there no longer, yet
when then with increasing anxiety, almost frantic, disproportionately agitated
                              I searched for it,
thinking back I realized an unease.
I had sensed a blankness at my shoulder or
the absence of caesura, a de-articulation of my path's definition
that translated into an excessive continuity of my movement itself
subjectively equivalent to an acceleration
getting my motion even closer to a fall.

But what, as though on behalf of the object, made me truly uneasy:
I had not realized, for quite a while, that what I missed was missing, or even
what it was I was missing.
It seemed to indicate an inward emptiness.

An opening had disappeared, an instant flash of life, a white gesture in the stone.


                              (In memoria, Bett's Bakery.)

Holding though everything is already all busy about him his blanket
still folded about his head the homeless man as his white otherwise non-colored contemporaries
conceptualize him
is holding the blanket together as he stands at the curb in front of him
its planes distended about him from shoulders to hand so that in a way as I approach
where he is
not quite discerning what it is he is holding in his visible hand and so inclining
to a supposition he is begging
abstractly viewed presents a very handsome abstract figure combining aspects of
a boat under sail, the nomad riding in the flowing
movement of his burnous
and a windmill's giant wheel's slow turn up to the sky wherefore I am
relieved
to see him smoking, the ashgrey white of a cigarette smoked almost down to the end
in the hand that in front of him lends such beauty to his brown nighttime blanket,
not a begging man's paper cup.  The old gentleman is enjoying a smoke.
And the blanket?  It is spring time and there is no need of it other than to shield
his solitude
from the street's awakening haste.

a numerous population of small men and women, Asiatics,
their language emanating
from their mouths in the hieroglyphs of ancient comic strips, in sharp dialogue
have taken over what other people had
called "groceries."  Behind mounds of splendid fruit in variants of the  spherical
sparkling in an array of colors as distinctive as that of pleasure craft
they have set up the secret centers of their enterprise, salad bars
catering to the lonely.  The empire has desiccated the nation into a structure of
                                                    transactions
circulating wages.

The man, a certain size, turns his shoulder against the faint hint at a
                              checkerboard pattern
of the sidewalk's broken perspective in the rain smoked space with my eye
inexplicably in a parabola averting itself from him in its intake of him
turning back forward for the reason of habit not balance merely, lariat dragging
                              the image of the torque of his jacket
ahead of me as though by a swing of my second eye akin to his incidental turning
                              back toward no matter what or nothing
stepping off the curb through he may just have been standing there his body immersed
                              in his mind's incessant chatter of business
as is mine beneath the smoke veil of his memory outline: eye rolling on free play
                              ahead of my head, a gyrating ball of a body juggled
above the grid pattern of my mind's broken perspective, satin for fall.

I sometimes seem to perceive a blue space figured by a haze or a
discoloration assumed  for my eye hovering in the shape of a
small room vertically distended despite its indistinctness geometrically exact and
                                         rectilinear very high
above my elbow or my shoulder off to the side above the pavement almost
behind my back but such that my shoulder or elbow are within it as flowers might be
                                         partially
in the air above a table in a painting transparent to the buildings across the street
with nothing going on except perhaps some slight shifts
or perturbances of density, seeming, though not unreal not real either,
indication perhaps of some ambiguity of my location on the pavement
or suggestion of a possibility of escape, and by its quality
faintly upsetting to thought of which as an object of memory
                                         rather than of perception
it is an object not personal but merely an infoliation of the world's busy
                                         space, an
abstract, invisible and geometric, configuration
of emptiness, and in this regard
kind.

Walking the streets these mornings I see people.  I don't hear them.
At night returning, their sound surrounds them largely.

By now after some years
of destitution in the streets
seeping in from nowhere
but now having been there,
a grime thicker
than the filth mostly there anyhow
a professionalism has developed, a caste system  one could say, were it not
for the strict savage individualism
of the individual figures, handling
a plentitude of black plastic bags
or carts, the supermarket kind, their metal grill high off the ground
and the low and squatting kind with little wheels, hard
to push, the old men pushing them
having to lean into them.  In olden days one saw the rag pickers, finders
of cast-off clothing, men with nervous eyes, hurrying
in competition with one another, to hit
the rich spots known to them ahead of the garbage crews, and the bag ladies,
old blowsy women resting on park benches
surrounded by supermarket bags, brown paper with twine handles, containing
                                        perhaps, their belongings,
spring blankets & winter coats, carton cover for survival.

But now these many-coated men out of Beckett, these grandiose ladies and
rag pickers
have disappeared like burglars, and the home-less have adopted the American figure,
the figure of the huckster.  Dawn
is awash with
entrepreneurs
wending their arrived-at routes of survival, at night & in the evening,
& at office-closing time.

There were for a while many
many beggars, whites in family
groups, or the timid black confidence men whose fathers
had been referred to as "negroes," extending
styrofoam greasy-spoon water cups
as numerous as hydrants, clutching
small bags containing
beer bottles.  There were
cartless men and women
carrying their bag
over their shoulder, the poorest of the poor, improvident adventurers,
among the wash outs
the most reckless, refusing to do their time.  I was astonished
at so much courage.  I miss the drunkards and crazy ones displaying their misfiture
as public gesture of refusal.  They no longer stand out or are gone,
culled.  The collectors of returnable cans and bottles
have taken over, ciphers
in the system's cycle of consumption.

Sweeping lo these many years
through these purlieus of destitution, a thin
edge of adventure, I have watched these mechanics drop by drop,
the explosions of individual fate twisted
slowly into institutions.

# ADDENDUM

I walk here and I don't have to
and I wasn't meant to, the houses about me always
perfectly clear.  No thread ties me to them, eyes only
that see and they sink into me
and the traffic too and the people
and never become mine
and don't touch me.  No question arises.
There is no question here of unkindness, only
that perfect stillness
twisting through me, the container of all this noise
and all these bits of color and immediately forgotten faces.
Yet I feel perfectly at home here.
So you see I am not even afraid
nor merely discontent,
but simply unnourished, myself not stirring ever,
an old man virginal.

This is the truth.

STEFAN BRECHT WAS BORN IN BERLIN, GERMANY, IN 1924, AND CAME TO AMERICA IN 1942. HE IS A DOCTOR OF PHILOSOPHY AND HAS BEEN A TEACHER, A WRITER ON THEATER, STEIN AND GOYA, AS WELL AS A LATE-NIGHT ACTOR. HE LIVES AND WORKS IN THE CHELSEA DISTRICT, MANHATTAN.

| | | |
|---|---|---|
| 1881471772 | 6/2/95 | DONALD BRECKENRIDGE |
| 193313223X | 8TH AVENUE | STEFAN BRECHT |
| 1881471942 | ACTS OF LEVITATION | LAYNIE BROWNE |
| 1933132221 | ALIEN MATTER | REGINA DERIEVA |
| 1881471748 | ANARCHY | MARK SCROGGINS |
| 1881471675 | ANGELUS BELL | EDWARD FOSTER |
| 188147142X | ANSWERABLE TO NONE | EDWARD FOSTER |
| 1881471950 | APO/CALYPSO | GORDON OSING |
| 1933132248 | APPLES OF THE EARTH | DINA ELENBOGEN |
| 1881471799 | ARC: CLEAVAGE OF GHOSTS | NOAM MOR |
| 1881471667 | ARE NOT OUR LOWING HEIFERS SLEEKER THAN NIGHT-SWOLLEN MUSHROOMS? NADA GORDON | |
| 0972066276 | BALKAN ROULETTE | DRAZAN GUNJACA |
| 1881471241 | BANKS OF HUNGER AND HARDSHIP | J. HUNTER PATTERSON |
| 1881471624 | BLACK LACE | BARBARA HENNING |
| 1881471918 | BREATHING FREE | VYT BAKAITIS (ED.) |
| 1881471225 | BY THE TIME YOU FINISH THIS BOOK YOU MIGHT BE DEAD AARON ZIMMERMAN | |
| 1933132299 | CLEOPATRA HAUNTS THE HUDSON | SARAH WHITE |
| 1881471829 | COLUMNS: TRACK 2 | NORMAN FINKELSTEIN |
| 0972066284 | CONVICTION & SUBSEQUENT LIFE OF SAVIOR NECK CHRISTIAN TEBORDO | |
| 1881471934 | CONVICTIONS NET OF BRANCHES | MICHAEL HELLER |
| 1881471195 | CORYBANTES | TOD THILLEMAN |
| 1881471217 | DANCING WITH A TIGER | ROBERT FRIEND |
| 1881471284 | DAY BOOK OF A VIRTUAL POET | ROBERT CREELEY |
| 1881471330 | DESIRE NOTEBOOKS | JOHN HIGH |
| 1881471683 | DETECTIVE SENTENCES | BARBARA HENNING |
| 1881471357 | DIFFIDENCE | JEAN HARRIS |
| 1881471802 | DONT KILL ANYONE, I LOVE YOU | GOJMIR POLAJNAR |
| 1881471985 | EVIL QUEEN | BENJAMIN PEREZ |
| 1881471837 | FAIRY FLAG AND OTHER STORIES | JIM SAVIO |
| 1881471969 | FARCE | CARMEN FIRAN |
| 188147187X | FLAME CHARTS | PAUL OPPENHEIMER |
| 1881471268 | FLICKER AT THE EDGE OF THINGS | LEONARD SCHWARTZ |
| 1933132027 | FORM | MARTIN NAKELL |
| 1881471756 | GENTLEMEN IN TURBANS, LADIES CAULS | JOHN GALLAHER |
| 1933132132 | GESTURE THROUGH TIME | ELIZABETH BLOCK |
| 1933132078 | GOD'S WHISPER | DENNIS BARONE |
| 1933132000 | GOWANUS CANAL, HANS KNUDSEN | TOD THILLEMAN |
| 1933132183 | HALF-GIRL | STEPHANIE DICKINSON |
| 1881471586 | IDENTITY | BASIL KING |
| 1881471810 | IN IT WHATS IN IT | DAVID BARATIER |
| 0972066233 | INCRETION | BRIAN STRANG |
| 1933132159 | INVERTED CURVATURES | FRANCIS RAVEN |
| 0972066217 | JACKPOT | TSIPI KELLER |
| 1881471721 | JAZZER & THE LOITERING LADY | GORDON OSING |
| 1881471926 | KNOWLEDGE | MICHAEL HELLER |
| 1933132310 | LADY V. | D.R. POPA |
| 193313206X | LAST SUPPER OF THE SENSES | DEAN KOSTOS |
| 1881471470 | LITTLE TALES OF FAMILY AND WAR | MARTHA KING |
| 0972066241 | LONG FALL | ANDREY GRITSMAN |
| 0972066225 | LYRICAL INTERFERENCE | NORMAN FINKELSTEIN |
| 1933132094 | MALCOLM & JACK | TED PELTON |
| 1933132086 | MERMAID'S PURSE | LAYNIE BROWNE |
| 1881471594 | MIOTTE | RUHRBERG & YAU (EDS.) |
| 097206625X | MOBILITY LOUNGE | DAVID LINCOLN |
| 1881471322 | MOUTH OF SHADOWS | CHARLES BORKHUIS |
| 1881471896 | MOVING STILL | LEONARD BRINK |
| 1881471209 | MS | MICHAEL MAGEE |
| 1933132302 | NO PERFECT WORDS | NAVA RENEK |
| 19331322-2 | NORTH & SOUTH | MARTHA KING |
| 1881471853 | NOTES OF A NUDE MODEL | HARRIET SOHMERS ZWERLING |

All Spuyten Duyvil titles are available through your local bookseller via *Booksense.com*

Distributed to the trade by
Biblio Distribution
a division of NBN
1-800-462-6420
*http://bibliodistribution.com*

All Spuyten Duyvil authors may be contacted at
*authors@spuytenduyvil.net*

Author appearance information and background at
*http://spuytenduyvil.net*